How ~~to~~ from a Stone

Priscila Uppal

TORONTO
Exile Editions
1998

Text Copyright © PRISCILA UPPAL 1998
Copyright © EXILE EDITIONS LIMITED 1998

All rights reserved. The use of any part of this publication, reproduced, transmitted in any form or by any means, electronic, mechanical, photocopying, recording or otherwise stored in a retrieval system, without the prior consent of the publisher is an infringement of the copyright law.

This edition is published by Exile Editions Limited, 20 Dale Avenue, Toronto, Ontario, Canada   M4W 1K4

Sales Distribution:
McArthur & Company
c/o Harper Collins
1995 Markham Road
Toronto, Ontario
M1B 5M8
800 387 0117

Layout and Design by MICHAEL P. CALLAGHAN
Composed and Typeset at MOONS OF JUPITER, Toronto
Printed and Bound by AMPERSAND PRINTING, Guelph
Cover & Author's Photographs by CHRISTOPHER DODA

The Canada Council
Conseil des Arts du Canada

The publisher wishes to acknowledge the assistance toward publication of the Canada Council and the Ontario Arts Council.

ISBN 1-55096-230-2

I would like to thank all those who have made this book possible: Barry Callaghan, for his editing and encouragement; Branko Gorjup for his inspiration; Richard Teleky and Rosemary Sullivan for their reading and support; Annie and David Layton for their home and advice; all friends and family, especially George Murray and Shannon Bramer for past publishing, reading, and their enormous passion; and Christopher Doda, in particular, for his always open eyes, ears, and love.

Some of these poems first appeared in *Exile The Literary Quarterly*, and *Beetred-a journal of poetry*.

for those creatures who want to see in the dark

Section 1 – *created*

How to Draw Blood from a Stone   *13*

When god created   *14*

Weaving   *15*

Porches   *16*

In My Neighbourhood   *18*

Tulips   *19*

The Revolt of the Weeds   *20*

Those Men   *21*

Death   *22*

The Art of Replacement   *23*

Through Your Veins   *24*

Possible Camping Encounter   *25*

There is us   *26*

The Retired Orchestra   *28*

What Birds Dream of   *29*

Fellatio   *30*

The Politics of Water   *31*

How Women Mourn   *33*

Warning to a Gynecologist   *35*

Section 2 – *collapsed*

Theory   *39*

Palms   *40*

Broken   *42*

Fireflies   *43*

Butterflies   *45*

When god collapsed   *46*

The Fall   *48*

How Stars Make Love   *49*

Angels Sleeping   *50*

careful careful   *51*`

Orbits   *52*

Inadequacy   *53*

Keep up   *55*

The Politics of Fire   *57*

Shedding   *58*

Downpour   *59*

Visiting Hours   *61*

Fatherless Angels   *62*

She returns   *63*

The Present   *64*

Bone-marrow   *65*

Section 3 – *died*

It's not your life that worries me   69

Tinted Glasses   70

when birds shake   71

Thanksgiving   72

Eulogy   73

Ghosts   74

The Squirrel's Dilemma   75

Uncles and Comas   76

When god died   77

Supposed to Be a Game   78

Grieving for mother   80

Cement Dolls   81

Blue are the ribs of the wrecked rowboat   82

An Apology for Dying Young   83

Cold   84

He explains the flower by the fertilizer   85

The Dead   86

The Third Fate   87

created

How to Draw Blood from a Stone

On family afternoons
the digging begins.
It begins with your hands.

You carry the stones like stillborn babies,
lay them down.
So closely the heads rise
from brown wet beds.

You add others when it rains,
when you're sad.
You name them all
by holding them down.

In winter they sit patiently
amongst the cold.
You stare wondering
what they want,
so close to the earth
and still.

This is not a place you go to speak.
The stones bleed through
the soil.

This is not a graveyard.
You can't apologize.

When god created

A latch-key kid from the beginning
he was a lonely child
the kind who needs imaginary friends
just to get by,
afraid of the dark.

Left alone for a week
he pushed the floor from the ceiling
drew plants and fruit on the walls
when he got hungry
counted the days and nights
through his window.

He saw winged creatures
and sea-monsters on his blankets
beasts and cattle on hardwood tables
filled the air with other children
and multiplied
multiplied
with every worried breath.

He heard his heart out loud.
He saw that it was good and
rested while creatures sniffed
the earth and fought.

On the eighth day he rubbed his eyes
forgot the universe made up in a corner
of his bedroom
and played only with stars.

Weaving

she can sit for hours
spinning invisible wool
her feet moving back and forth
on the rug instead of a pedal

it was her mother's craft
and now it's hers and I,
her daughter, she thinks I'm
the maid when I bring her tea

we read the leaves
telling fortunes in shapes
of green her shawl hanging
over her immaculately placed

when she's done knitting
she just sits and I wonder
how her back rests straight
as the chair how she can

gaze out the window and not
notice my hand in hers
mesmerized by a single drop
on the glass until bedtime

Porches

At the party my brother
was coaxed onto the piano
as I was led to the porch
by my Uncle's frothy breath
sweet on the wooden steps
his bruised hands sanded
and laid down last
August as I watched
and served his drinks.

Wondering how I looked
in the hand-me-down cotton
dress my aunt Lucy his wife
gave me if I could fill it in
and through the drapes
I caught her smile our neighbour's
hand resting on her knee.

"I don't know how to play."
The piano, I meant, jealous
of talents movements my
body couldn't perform.
The silly dances I used to do
for him in full make-up and
old hats a wet bath mat
I'd wear as a skirt.

He said he missed our cousin
Toby who died the spring
before and I was singing
"His hand caressed the arch
of her back" a line I found
dangerous inside my twelve-year-
old head and then he did
his hand sliding underneath
my first bra a gaze
inside the curtains asking
"You must be cold?"

I wasn't but wondered if
I should be.

In My Neighbourhood

In my neighbourhood
once a year we gather
for a burning.

Each brings a branch
a swatch of cloth
a painted set of eyes.

Leaves line our
driveways in crisp
shades of fire.

We chant options
of attack and brew
sugared kerosene.

Smell the inside of
your toaster. This is
how our street tastes.

We are waiting for
our children to
arrive.

Tulips

When you shed the skins
of your old life, you will
find me amongst the dead
heads of tulips, planted
in the backyard learning
through others how to return.

Be precise and carefully paced.
Even in direct light we bloom
only once a year
with barely enough time
to shine.

The Revolt of the Weeds

they trained all winter

their rebellion was nuclear

there were no casualties

this time there will be no mistakes

they will take hostages

Those Men

You thought those men hid
in closets or under the bed
with spiralling red eyes
and long scaly fingers, waiting
for a dangling foot or unguarded neck.

You slept with the lights on
or covers over your head. At slumber
parties you whispered about them,
sensing safety in groups.

Falling off a cliff in a dream,
waking with a start meant they had been there.
Close.
It would be those eyes that stayed in you
and the heat of melting.

Twenty years later and you know better.
The closet is for clothes.
You hide letters underneath the bed.

They are the eyes
that wink at you.
They are the eyes
that say
trust me.

Death

A slow word
like a crack on a teacup

The Art of Replacement

I've never replaced things before,
you know that. I kept the dresser with
the missing drawer (ripped in a moment of passion
I recall) and the sharp glass of the smashed lamp
tucked behind my books.

All gone now. I shipped in white wood
to fill in what had left, or what was too old
to keep around. I even built the shelves myself
(calluses to prove it) and no longer do I find socks
or the crescent shapes of your glasses or the smell
of one of your magazines underfoot.

It wasn't hard once I gained momentum to rid
myself of all that junk, the tired and the weary
I coddled for years. Even the picture frames
were easy to shove into bags and push to the curb.

At night in a wrought-iron bed (new too!)
I stretch out new sheets in white (I never had white
sheets before) like a woman frozen in the snow.

But it was just like you to appear when I least
wanted you. How could you, one night, just reach
out your fingers and pull open my drawers,
staining the new lining with your personals?

I walk among the dressers and coffee tables
revel in their smoothness, corners straight, finished,
and clean. Let me live in replacement. Let the past be
forced back on its own.

Through Your Veins

Veins rise from your skin,
a map of mountains and streams.
When you sleep my lips rest upon
one that ripples over your collarbone

a steady pulse of rain or snow
I capture on my tongue.
I try to infuse each layer, steep
inside your absent father, epileptic cousin,

find a similar taste for gin.
To be planted and born again
waking with your soil,
consumed, breathing blood through

an umbilical cord caught deep
in my throat.

Possible Camping Encounter

Camping we avoid the outhouse
at all costs. It is more satisfying
to squat in the woods, palms
down lifting our vertebrae to shelter
in a half-moon the buried
secrets of our food. Returning
our fig-leaves to Eden, wind taking
refuge in flesh, in a tornado brewing
from an eye. Tickled by a sliver of
grass, the pained marks of burr-bites
on skin, nose to the ground, we pant
in expectation. Why do we perform
this ritual in separate spots when I've
licked your body clean like our cat
at home on the couch and already
know you don't always smell like roses?
Naked from the waist down, I pump
myself closer to the dirt hoping you will
see me and waddle over with your pants
around your ankles, mount me from behind.
Then we could do like the animals, tails raised
in pride, sniff the air announcing
something vital has passed between us.

There is us
(for Shannon Bramer)

There is you on the steps
holding your flower handbag
waving good-bye dressed
in a V-cut business suit
hair swept up caught
by a wooden butterfly
and all I can see are phases
of you. One in pigtails
playing hopscotch where you
always picked the smoothest
light-gray stones. Later
in Irish pubs pounding
back B52s making me
laugh as you told me about eggs
how your boyfriend didn't make
you eggs like he used to
and that night we held
hands crying because we couldn't
help our drunk fathers
anymore and we shared memories
of lovers so long gone
we could barely describe
their faces then wanted to so bad
we raided yearbooks and photo albums
then said fuck it dancing 'til dawn.

There is you on the steps
holding your flower handbag
waving good-bye and me
knowing you in a different way
than before knowing
the next time we meet
I will have missed a phase
you will have missed one of mine.

The Retired Orchestra

Once a year at night the home on Queen Street
becomes a symphony. My grandfather,
probably an oboe, should be in this home.
He never passed up a dance with a lady
or the chance to sing a round.

They steal away from numbered rooms
and meet in the cafeteria. All the instruments tuned up
scaling their throats and shaking off
dust from their strings.

Large-bellied basses set the tone. Trombones clear
away tables, call in the flutes and the violins,
women with pursed lips who finger the air and sway.
Turned trays are drums, soup cans from the trash
become a xylophone, newcomers play the spoons
and conductors stand keeping the beat with sugar drips
sucked like long flat reeds.

Legs kick between sets—some whistle
and hoot, throw up their hands or pills, grab the arm
of the one beside them, unplug the clock,
spill salt shakers until the curtain of dawn
arises.

In the morning nurses and orderlies will wake
struggling with a hum from their dreams
as the orchestra retires to bed for another year
the fierce and strong notes that have held on
for a lifetime.

What Birds Dream of

Who hasn't dreamt of flying?
To sprout wings like buds
open to the sun and lifted
by the breath of an atmosphere.

It is a dream, flying, the moments
you catch before letting go
like mumbled prayers
to those who visit while you sleep.

Get away! they tell you as you fall
your arms waving at the world
spun with threads of others
disguised in the darkness.

It's the wind we want to befriend
the lovers of rescue we need
because we can't do it elsewhere
because we let ourselves be held.

But birds with two-way clocks
dream the heads of ostriches
stuck in the sand
glued in fright to the land.

They dream of clipped wings and
vacuums and lone flocks without
instinct, of finding one place
in the world to stand, just to stand.

Fellatio

I'm sculpting a tiny death
in my potter's wheel
your skin ripples in motion
in time with the hum

Water is used to soften
the unformed clay
my lips knead and
mould a living wave

An exercise in timing
to link hand with heat
once in the kiln
every flaw will show

A suicide art moving
with a cry into me
and I'm left with tears
of a crouching child.

I wonder why I worked
so hard just to empty you
to have what I shaped
slip down from my hands

The Politics of Water

Our bodies were made
in a wash tub. Water
broke our olive skins
into bubbles and we
rose red as blisters
just as fragile
perhaps more painful.

When bodies turn in
hot water the mouth
stays open. Legs
flex, relax.
Lips wrap around
hooks and pull
back down.

We held each other
like seaweed
the rush of currents
made us want
to dive underneath.

Retrieve old skins
hold them to light
offer a quick breath
to newly formed curves
in the hollow of a tub
the finest creatures have
broken their shells.

"Our bodies were made
to fly" I said and my hands
skimmed across your
layered bones and missed.
You were already drowning.
And the water held you
closer than I could.

How Women Mourn
    (in response to C.Weissman Wilks' sculptures)

Women mourn with their hands.
Without something to hold
fingers stretch uneasily
as if re-learning how to walk
tentative yet deliberate movements.

Women mourn with their eyes.
Begging on their knees to the sky
to break itself and drop all
they've lost back into their laps.
They believe in miracles.

Because there are never reasons
to satisfy the crippling space
men mourn with their anger
making their home a picture
of all that frightens them.

When a woman mourns sometimes
she finds herself in an attic
her dress tied behind her
and hands soaked in water
with every bottle in the house.

A man takes a walk searching
for streets he can no longer name.
A woman will sculpt the attic
into others made of glass.
They mourn in colour.

And sometimes a woman mourns
by inviting another woman
to touch her fragile figures
find the one hairlessly draped
over the hole by her abdomen.

Unable to cradle her flesh
women mourn the children.
Trapped inside her belly,
they believe, lives everyone
you've ever loved.

Warning to a Gynecologist

Remember that you have seen further than many:

Tested the waters;
Canals, escape routes, and waterfalls,
Visions of the red sea.

From an open sea-shell you've heard
An ocean in waiting.

Chart the territory with a prophet's diligence.

Be careful what you take:

You could push away kin almost forgotten
Or dislodge an angel I buried in the field.

collapsed

Theory

When the earth was flat
you were wary of travel.

Now your fear is circular.

That you will find nowhere
but home.

Palms

The Fool cups the world
in his hands, arms raised with eyes
up, a foot sliding over a cliff.

My mother inherited foresight
from her mother.
She has learned to deal
with one hand, and the kitchen
revolves over her fingers like
the flame of the candle beside her.

She knows about lines
on hands and fists.
Which lines to cross
and which to not.

Clothes packed and unpacked
shuffled and misplaced, her family
heirlooms hidden in her sleeves.

She tells me time is no fool.
The world is not a wound-up clock
forgotten and waiting to stop.

Lines predict weather,
a storm or drizzle of visitors
in patterns, and here, in a kitchen
with her agile fingers, I believe her.

The door opens and slams.
The candle blows out.
Dinner is late.

In the morning her face
spread by fingerprints.
My grip on her body, her palm on the burner,
erasing the life she doesn't want,
me clinging to her sliding feet.

Broken

When mother threw the vase
at father's chest I saw flesh
was not tangible. He loved her
despite the stitches.

And later the groans would
pass there could be laughter
or tears. From where I was
they sounded the same.

(Love that is broken is understood
by children, somewhere between
the schoolyard and the bedroom
a scraped knee and spread legs.

The stitches we carry natural
as sleep, those same stars
unraveling, our tiny fingers
grazing over a delicate face.)

There were soft touches
misleading as feathers and fists
hard as gold locks, mostly
opened and then forgotten.

It is the way I mistook mother's
eyes when she smoothed cream
over bruises. The way she stared
eclipsed by the stars.

Fireflies

It took my father four days
to realize she was gone.

He checked the furniture
the plants outside against his map
of where things belong
and came up with nothing
but disappearance.

I was the one who told him
check the accounts
look in the cabinets
her hairnet is missing
and all the loose change.

The hearts of mothers who leave
are kept in bell jars
like fireflies
beating furiously against the glass
electric.

Under a summer sun
I cut the lawn
froze garden vegetables
fed the dogs
and washed the windows.

Behind the veranda he stared
at flypaper
his skin burned
like a meteorite
the barbecue left unattended.

He glues letters to the fridge
keeps out of the way
of trees and storms
locks the doors
searches for a pin-hole to breathe through.

Butterflies

you told me to be careful
with your butterfly brooch
the aquamarine one
with red tulip cased stones
you wore on Sundays
with a straw sun hat

sometimes we lose things
when we don't pay attention
we break a wing
we misplace a stone
it slips between our fingers
before a thought can pass
then it's lost

I kept an eye on it every second
as I pranced around the house
pretending I was you
in black heels and
thick red lipstick
one of your faded dresses
hiked up in my tiny hands

I still have that brooch
curl it delicately between fingers
wings and stones intact
it was you that slipped by me
broken without attention
with barely a sound

When god collapsed

He was trying to catch
His runaways,
Make up for lost time.
"I've wasted so many
Years," he said.

But all the houses were unfamiliar,
And alleyways narrow.
Not used to the cold
Or the noise,
He ran out of breath.

A few minutes late
An ambulance arrived at the corner
He lost sight of his children, thinking
Someone must have snatched them
Thrown them into a passing car.
He was waving his arms
For a cab to beat them to the airport.

They lifted him.
"Lost a lot of blood,"
He heard.

And the lights were white and blinding.
And the doors swung open as a sky.

"My children," he howled.
"I need my children!"
They strapped him down,
Worried about shock.

Bystanders crowded around the lights
That night, watching the old man, and
Healers at work, trying to figure
Out if they knew him, or if anyone
Should be notified.

The Fall

Adam knew the leaves would fall
and Eve did the picking.

Cursed with bareness the ground
gave its own back like tears.

Coloured veins that burst
with the vengeance of children.

They were too many to account for.
Not enough to forgive.

We are always to blame for winter.
Its coming and its leaving.

The trees remember as statues
waiting to be flowered.

Eve with her basket of fruit
and Adam with his of futility.

Every nine months we are forced
to remember the warmth gone.

Every nine months we are forced
to collect the dead and move on.

How Stars Make Love

Not so quickly as one might think.
In the sky everything takes time—
there's so much space to travel.

They're afraid we might be watching
through a telescope or one of those probes,
so they wait perfectly still
shining in their loneliness.

Wearing dresses of sequins,
stars ache for daylight
wave their lashes through the milky way
pout with lips of burnt candy.

Millions of years between them before
they touch, stars are shy of contact
creep back to safe places
parts of town they know best
until they're almost too old to care.

It's the last light that streaks the sky
when stars make love
right before they die

hey you, fella, hang on to me
please hold me tight,
I'm just about to fall—

Angels Sleeping

They sleep in corners of closets and cracks of cupboards
    back seats in buses huddled with young widows
    basement apartments in downtown Toronto
    outside lottery ticket stands in early morning
    vegetable peddlers in summer and
    underneath liquor stores in winter
    with knotted hair and callused feet and pink lipstick
    with white handbags and choir sheets taped to their cheeks
    and a blanket they don't mind sharing.

They wait against slamming doors and bottles
    bumps and bruises worn while travelling
    hot air that sneaks out barred windows
    outside for change or cigarettes
    fresh cucumbers or baskets to hold
    when the carolers swing by
    with hands outstretched and tired legs and pink roses
    with white eyes and numbers stitched to their clothes
    and a begging they don't mind calling love.

Wake up angels, don't make me repeat myself.
Pick up your things, and move along.

careful careful

if you drop this poem
it won't forgive you
won't return even one
of your calls it will
pass you by on the street
looking the other way
with shades on and heeled
shoes and never will it
trust you again or lie
in your arms or care if
you cry or even stop to
watch you fall it has no
time for you if you can't
hold for just a second
wait for it to adjust
to the bumps in your hands
remember if you drop this
poem with certainty
it will never admit it
ever loved you, not to anyone

Orbits
(for Gwendolyn MacEwen)

Outside my basement apartment
on Robert Street I read your voice
and don't ask for light when it falls
squinting to find you
in your darkness
as if the woman would orbit free
of the page
until my eyes turn into seeds
and I must glimpse you in sunlight

Inadequacy

I have not thought about this poem long enough
to write it well.
I am confessing
my inadequacy,
every word used against me.

If I had known that would be the last time
I would have let you peel off strips of skin
    wrap my hair in turbans
    pour kerosene on my thighs
until our mouths spit out ashes.

I would have stapled your limbs to the floor
    traced your body onto paper
    coloured outside of the lines
a cheap souvenir to paste
to wink at from my dirty mattress.

I would have cut off your eyelashes
and pasted them like dandelion petals
    on my toes
and let you sleep peacefully.

I would have made the imprint into a
crossword puzzle
    'til we found words to fit
in the square over your bellybutton
I would write the letter Z with my come.
I am not good
at saying good-bye
and this can be used against me.

I would not have spilt tears as I did.
I would have left a waterfall
    on your crass pubic hair
I would have savoured the taste
of you—your come—seeping
out like liquid paper erasing
the moments before they could be
contained.

Of course,
I did not know it would be the last time
and all the would have's I use
against you.

Keep up

I was usually a turn behind
taking time to browse in shop windows
and wave at faces passing by.
I stopped for strangers
and read street name signs.
Keep up, my father would say,
disappointed in my slowness.
My brother who walked in bursts
grew tall from his long strides.

Walking fast all I noticed
were the prints of my feet.
With no time for love,
not the kind that lingers,
not the kind that plants you.

My father would grab hold of my arm.
Soon I didn't struggle.
I knew I had to get going.
People who were strangers, stayed strangers
left by the turn of a heel.

Letting go of you has been harder.
The girl I used to be is with you.
Her skin unravels in my backward glance
into thin bones and elbows resting
on a ribcage, hands clasped as if in prayer.
Our fingers stretch like parting clouds.

Looking ahead I know she has stumbled
lost at a turn behind. And it's not your eyes
as abandoned, that hurt me. Or the knowledge
of my own heart failing. It's how my legs
can't wait to move further and further away
when I'd rather linger.

The Politics of Fire

My mother burned our house
down when I was twelve. Only
the trees bent back to see
the walls crumble.

I let my children play
with matches, to understand
the discipline it takes to
cover before striking.

Shedding

Blind in the darkness of linoleum caves
    he tries to conquer
    she merely tries
slippery fingers searching for what was lost

    an hour ago—a year ago

Continually shedding one body for another
    apocalyptic dancers
    forgetting the steps they never knew
mourning after the storm.

Downpour

I didn't want to give flowers without the soil
But his window is eclipsed by the west wing.
'That's the cancer ward,' he tells me. 'Some of those lights
stay on all night.'

We made alternate decisions.
First by the window, where
It could be touched by feathery light, yet my father
Couldn't see or smell the bulbs
Over creams and cleansers.

We switched to the bedside
Hoping lamplight would be enough,
That it could stretch against the odds.

Finally it was placed on the windowsill
Away from corners, not too close, the midway
Point between us and outside.

We talk of the weather, it's why I don't call.
I don't want to ask how you are, what the weather's like
Up there.

'The rain,' I tell him, 'Means somewhere above
a woman's giving birth.'
He asks me to rub his back, keep talking.
So I do.

The mornings I sleep over, the sun hits his face
Like a pillow, eyelids lift sheets away.
I bring him water.

I push the button on the bed and my father
Is raised up to face me. 'It's stopped raining,' I tell him.
He says, 'The west wing always shines in the morning.'

The three of us watch out the window
Twisting our spines and reaching for sky.

Visiting Hours

he wants to know
who the short guy is
who talks too much

that's your son
they tell him
his name is Peter

he doesn't quite remember
how he got here
or why he can't recall his bed

he remembers the street name
where he lived until twelve
he thinks he lives there still

he thinks the blond girl
who brought flowers must be his daughter
she is a granddaughter

he is nervous tonight
tells the nurse
a beautiful woman is coming

he knows that much
he doesn't know she's his wife

"I'd go anywhere but hell
to see that smile," he says.
She already has.

Fatherless Angels

They are almost all fatherless these days,
unless they have many,
their eyes fallen like seeds from sunflowers
or daffodils, yellow and
drifting

I've seen them with their wings stretched wide
jumping in front of cars
with signs on their backs and luggage stuffed
between feathers.
They don't care where they go,
they just want to go somewhere else.

All the street maps to heaven are sold
wrapped in plastic
directions to movie stars and palm trees
hot in their hands, sweaty and flat
like lottery tickets.

I was stabbed by an angel once,
right in my side
when I wasn't looking.
Neither was he.
Sorry, he said, I thought
you were my dad.

She returns

I will not look at you straight on.
As a child you warned me:
Never face an eclipse,
It will burn your eyes.

The Present

It was difficult to speak
of the past last night.
You no longer looked
like a cracked vase.

Behind you I needed
to see the woman who hid us
in closets with the other animals.
Who took blows against the
door, served my father her thin
body on platters. We too
picked at scraps.

Underneath the table
I counted shards of glass
to calm myself the way I count
days between visits.
I kept one in my shoe.

When we speak of the past
words growl between held hands
until sleepy, crawl towards
a washroom and silent bandages
the click of a door shut
during a storm.

'I would have done things
differently,' you say.
I forgive you. Things would
have been exactly the same.

Bone-marrow

Trees know each other by their bark.
Everything alive has developed a language.
Even thunder, even death.

Children are obsessed with mirrors
trying to pry the glass free
to release the twin who understands their every move
and face.

Lovers despair the moment
they no longer find a reflection
in each other's tears.

Look at science:
Desperately in love with itself searching
for solar systems identical to ours.
Signs of life.

For want of bone-marrow
the entire kingdom was lost.

Think about why religions fail.

died

It's not your life that worries me

Stones can be visited. Darkness
Is the only place worth candles.

Light one, if you can. If there is
Light there, tell me, where you are
What does water taste like? In which
Direction does the sun set? And are
You shivering?

Tinted Glasses

Mine were made by my careful father.
I see faults in construction,
sense failure of hands
in the world of weather and sands.
But still I work,
and work, until only I know the blunders.

You were given broken lenses.
Everything smashed.
Destroyed before able to flower,
dead before giving birth.
I knew how badly you grieved for life
as you saw it dying.
I knew how your waist-side fell.

Beyond glass is the air,
the space your arms reach to in the dark.
We move as if crying.
We move with the gentleness of breakage.

Here is where confessions are useless.

Here is where I lay my glasses
afraid the strain has caused damage
only

I tell you sweet, you know,
you know how love ends
the fear of rotting
and glass makes us seem further away.

when birds shake

not the trembling with cold
in winter, it's the shiver
of a schoolmate who's died
that we haven't thought of
in years

Thanksgiving

As you hold the carving knife
we bow our heads and close our eyes
out of grace and comfort.

We give thanks for:
the bird
the candles
the silver spoons
I will one day inherit.

You tell stories about the dog
all the time thinking there are not
enough rolls and too much
plum pudding.

No one mentions the one less spot
this year.

No one answers the knock at the door.

Eulogy

It would be consolation
to believe you were dead and gone
instead of alive and not here
that I could rain petals on your stone
recite poetry to a corpse.

I could wear black dresses
(trailing on the earth)
and knit lace
to wear you as a veil
to shield my eyes.

Instead of knowing you continue
in a space I am denied access
whispers I will never hear
and women you will enter
like a spy
to find information I could not provide.

Ghosts

All the lies you were told
about the ways of ghosts.
They don't come out at night.
Nor do they scream or cry
or crave your body.

No doors knock or windows rattle.
Nothing moves.
They are always there.
The secret of ghosts
is how they disappear,
start a new life—
get out of the house.

You keep the kitchen spotless.
Fresh flowers on the window sill,
porch lamps lit, and hands flat
as the table where you sit
praying for the phone to ring.

You don't dare sleep in case
you miss him. Waiting the way
you did during the war:
for a white light—a hand—someone
you could follow away.

The Squirrel's Dilemma

When your time comes
with all the places to turn
or hideaways that have become
comfortable, do you cower?
Or does your body stiffen
trusting the light to lift you
believing in those enormous bright eyes?

Uncles and Comas

Just like being drunk, he said,
another year I can't remember.

We marvelled at my aunt who never
left though she promised to
and every year we told her
we didn't blame her, or him.

I couldn't after the coma, she said,
who knows where he's been?

We suspected tunnels and
bright lights and other hands
pulling him closer, voices
telling him not to return.

Heaven's like any other place,
my mother added, some man
telling you to be happy and forget.
A coma's no different.

Except he cried in the coma.

When god died

Sure, the madmen predicted it,
But no one took them seriously.

The priests had no idea.
Just another body to deliver,
Some people to comfort.

It made the local news:
A child who needed a transplant.

And some opened their purses,
Emptied out what was left at the end
Of the month.

A few joined the family,
left flowers at the graveyard.
Thinking they hadn't really
known him, god willing,
They might have.

The new heart, unfortunately, was rejected.
The madmen wept uncontrollably.

People said the usual things:
He could've been something
Could've had the world at his feet
That kid didn't even get a chance.

Supposed to Be a Game

We thought it was funny
to grab the girl we called Bucky
because of her crooked teeth
and tie her with skipping rope
to a tree with a promise of rescue
if she stood still

She peed her pants and we ran
(who was with me I can't remember)
she had to call for a neighbour
to take her home with wet jeans
and marks on her wrists
the next day I wouldn't sit
beside her on the bus

we played the Lady of Shalott,
Sleeping Beauty, Anne Boleyn;
we played hangings, drownings,
hidden rooms of treasured bones;
we played dead

We thought it would be brave
to take turns in an open grave
it wasn't even midnight
reading stones for enticing bodies
we could possess for the day
we liked the ones who died young

my turn and my face loose lips
left open and arms crossed neatly
dirt cushioning my neck as
the others sang prayers with hands
interlocked and between giggles
I peeked to make sure they were there
they teased me when spiders crawled
over my shirt and I ran out embarrassed
not waiting to cry until safe at home

Yesterday a group of children playing
chicken with the 2 o'clock train
found a girl's body in a ditch
(the details are unimportant)
an after-concert party gone too far
empty beer bottles and unfastened
belt buckles torn-out brown hair
with no apparent struggle except
that she stood still

In this room the rules of
recess come back to me in verse
a band of bodies with hands
and tragic imaginations
the walk home's a little quicker
after dark this winter the echo
of a child's laughter coming suddenly
to a halt.

Grieving for mother

it took months to put together
clues of lost luggage and plane tickets
the hotel lobby we received a postcard
wish you were here it began

we made plans for funerals
my brother dressed in black
and I sang until my voice broke
while underneath the piano
my father cut photographs

though my mother wasn't a puzzle
we clipped her clothes
hung her jewellery from bannisters
until our home became a museum

everything was clear and concrete
her departure only sudden
if viewed from the point
of family myth

I dreamt she thanked me
for the kind words and lovely song
she had hoped for flowers
but mothers are always pleased
with their children

only when I looked in the mirror
did I find my mother's eyes
and the rage of my father
caught in my smile

Cement Dolls

Underneath the street
where the subway rides
are little girls in red dresses
who scrape the floors
(the ones you're not
supposed to cross)
looking for signs.

They dig up legs
and arms, a lip sometimes
two and put them in their
baskets, trot along the
metal wires never stepping
on a crack.

Underneath the street
where the subway rides
the girls play house
and scrape the floors
(the ones they know
you never cross)
digging up signs.

Blue are the ribs of the wrecked rowboat
(for Virginia Woolf)

The blue ink of your pen
spilled over the sea.
The lighthouse drew you.
A clear beam in the darkness
sturdy as your portrait.

Shadow swarming blue
with a pocketful of stones
weighted words clasped
in taut palms your
tired oars floating.

One of your children
moulded from the ribs
of your wrecked rowboat.
Blue as the stones
I collect from the shore.

An Apology for Dying Young

I was made
of sheet lightning
which is why my life
was shockingly short.

If you look closely
you can still see my coded
poems in the sky,
unsigned.

Cold

I will never get used to walking
with my head down and fingers cramped
in pockets, with a wool hat I wear because
it is familiar and warm. Stumbling
stiff, careful not to slip or let any skin
show, making a path for home,
gazing briefly at streetlights
as faces blow by.

Decorating the walkway in tinsel
and bright red bows
like the letters I keep safe
from loved ones who have died.

This is the season they return.
Under snow, bones frozen from
a banal fall, begging for a blanket,
a touch without gloves, telling me
not to step outside with my hair wet,
without clear directions, and eyes
that melt Spring all over
my windows.

He explains the flower by the fertilizer

Last night I tried to tell him about a flower
that grew because it wanted to see
the sky, a flower whose leaves curled outward
from a slab of stone.

Last night I wrapped myself around him
and held after the man had chased me
trying to tear my dress and I want him to understand
that I didn't do that because I was afraid
I did it because I was free.

The Dead

We are the guardians of angels.
Get down on your knees, push
your hands into the earth. Smell
the sweet stench of angels and listen:
they don't whisper, they scream.
Dig the hard dirt around you,
This is the promised land.

The Third Fate

When the time comes you will
be led to your bed.

The midwife will arrive and
a bell to ring for water.

Skin will sink stitched
into eyes and bone.

Two sisters will abandon you.
You will have no father.

All loose threads will be tied.

She will take your knitted life
and lay it on top of you.

You will begin to see symmetry
in the dark.

A mother's voice will say:

You have lived long enough
in this form.

Here is your cocoon:
Become a butterfly.